human nature

Maria Asuncion

BookLeaf Publishing

Presentation by *BookLeaf Publishing*

Web: www.bookleafpub.com

E-mail: info@bookleafpub.com

ISBN: 9789395756792

First edition 2022

DEDICATION

To my Hub, with the ferocity of immense and
all-encompassing love.

ACKNOWLEDGEMENT

I'm not one to highlight my strengths, but I am very good at being very grateful. So I'd like to acknowledge the many wonderful folks who have supported me without hesitation.

Thank you so much to Ma and Ba for their never-ending admiration of my creativity. Thank you to my best friend, Li, who has always been my cheerleader for every event of my life.

Thank you to my found family in the Naruses, who unquestioningly provided me with a beautiful home, a safe and loving space, as well as the love of my life, Michael.

PREFACE

Wow, writing a poetry book! It's definitely a thrill in a way that's exhilaratingly happy yet nearly inexplicably scary. I suppose I'm writing this preface to try to explain why it's scary for me, but if I may, I'd love to start by introducing myself to you, dear reader whose time and energy I'm grateful for.

I'm Maria, and I've loved poems all my life, from silly limericks to Shakespearean sonnets. My love for English lit motivated me to study it during my undergrad at University of Toronto, and from there, my love for it kept growing. Though I loved it, I had trouble expressing my inner thoughts in creative writing, so I decided to teach English classes at a secondary and post-secondary level instead, and that's how I ended up pursuing my Master in Education, and eventually, I started working at Toronto Metropolitan University, where I've been for the past few years. My career as an educator has given me the lovely opportunity to support so many students, all of whom I've watched in awe overcome challenges again and again. The reason why I mention them is because they inspire me to speak my truth and not to be afraid of my inner thoughts, as I found myself encouraging them to do so, yet I had not been able to do it for so long myself.

Though I'm scared to share, I wanted to overcome that challenge by writing this book. This book is my way of sharing some of my inner thoughts, which I've written in the form of haiku, reflecting upon how as humans, we act similarly to many parts of nature. Think of our animal companions, the greenery around us, the bodies of water in the distance, the skies above, the ground beneath and the air around us. We alter them and are altered by them, yet sometimes this is achieved so subtly that we may not take the moment to recognize its impacts; just as I have for so long, with my students, with my friends and with my family. Sometimes, our actions and speech may seem small, but their influence ripples out further than we think. The action you thought was not as important has probably transformed someone's way of thinking. Asking someone how they're doing may have been a simple way to check in with them, yet they valued your interest in them and felt seen and heard.

I thought of such things while observing nature around me as I walked along with my spouse,

which is one of my most enjoyable activities.
My spouse and I have walked to and around
many parks, basking under the sun, as well as
enjoying the evening breeze. During those
walks, we'd see cute and funny things: squirrels
chatting wildly, dogs being silly, cats being
mystifying. There were also other little instances
I found fascinating, such as noticing how water
behaves at a rocky beach and how the breeze
carries a leaf. To me, all of it is not as simple as
it seems; just as you picking up this book is due
to your own reasons–perhaps curiosity, word of
mouth or simply chance–your action has left a
great impact on me.

distance

The sun sends rays from
far away, yet I feel its
warmth right next to me.

warm front

After a heat wave,
the wind blows cold but still holds
some warmth from summer.

harmony

3

A bird sings high notes.
The wind gusts a low bellow.
A surprising song.

share

A rabbit thumps, scared.
This exposes him, yet it's
how he shares bravely.

trees

My love walks with me.
Under the sun, we see
a sage tree. Maple.

heh

A dog is alert,
looking up at a tree, but
the squirrel's by its feet.

piece

A leaf falls slowly.
Gently, it lands in one piece
—crunch! Now, in pieces.

company

A squirrel twirls its tail,
settles well on a branch, and
cries for company.

company continued

Some sudden sounds, so
I look around and find two
squirrels chatting loudly.

reeds

The pond by the beach
has many reeds, hiding birds
premigratory.

stork

The stork is tall and
unassuming, letting pass-
-ersby pause in awe…

rocky beach

Waves crash on the rocks.
The rocks stay and receive the
embrace of the waves.

wall

'Why rocks at the beach?'
I ask my love, and he says,
'To slow erosion.'

gradual

A rock surrenders
To the torrent of high tides
Unmoved, eroding.

Y

15

A stream of water
splits into two, yet the stream
all falls the same way.

U

The breeze carries a
fallen leaf far away and
brings it back to me.

pup

17

A man walks his pup
without a leash. It runs off
worrying the man.

startle

A cat loudly cries,
startling me. She runs to me,
asking for comfort.

wind chill

19

The sun has set, so
now the breeze sends a chill down
my spine. Refreshing.

home

Metal chimes against
the wind. It means we are home.
Last glance at the sky.

full

The moon wanes, shyly
retreating into the skies.
It will return full.